COUNTRY PROFILES

POLAND

BY ALICIA Z. KLEPEIS

BLASTOFF! DISCOVERY

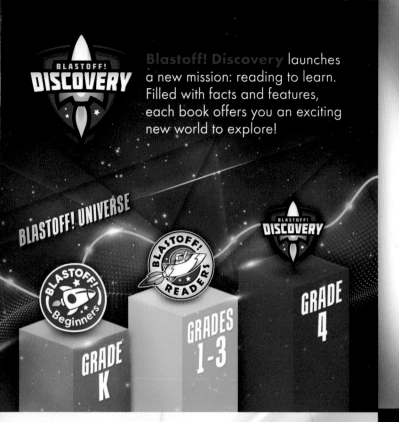

Blastoff! Discovery launches a new mission: reading to learn. Filled with facts and features, each book offers you an exciting new world to explore!

BLASTOFF! UNIVERSE

BLASTOFF! Beginners — GRADE K

BLASTOFF! READERS — GRADES 1-3

BLASTOFF! DISCOVERY — GRADE 4

This edition first published in 2022 by Bellwether Media, Inc.

No part of this publication may be reproduced in whole or in part without written permission of the publisher.
For information regarding permission, write to Bellwether Media, Inc.,
Attention: Permissions Department,
6012 Blue Circle Drive, Minnetonka, MN 55343.

Library of Congress Cataloging-in-Publication Data

Names: Klepeis, Alicia, 1971- author.
Title: Poland / by Alicia Z. Klepeis.
Description: Minneapolis, MN: Bellwether Media, 2022. |
   Series: Blastoff! Discovery: Country Profiles | Includes
   bibliographical references and index. | Audience: Ages 7-13 |
   Audience: Grades 4-6 | Summary: "Engaging images accompany
   information about Poland. The combination of high-interest subject
   matter and narrative text is intended for students in grades 3 through
   8." Provided by publisher.
Identifiers: LCCN 2021051758 (print) | LCCN 2021051759 (ebook)
   | ISBN 9781644876138 (library binding)
   | ISBN 9781648346248 (ebook)
Subjects: LCSH: Poland–Juvenile literature.
Classification: LCC DK4147 .K54 2022 (print) |
   LCC DK4147 (ebook) | DDC 943.8–dc23/eng/20211026
LC record available at https://lccn.loc.gov/2021051758
LC ebook record available at https://lccn.loc.gov/2021051759

Editor: Rachael Barnes   Designer: Brittany McIntosh

Printed in the United States of America, North Mankato, MN.

TABLE OF CONTENTS

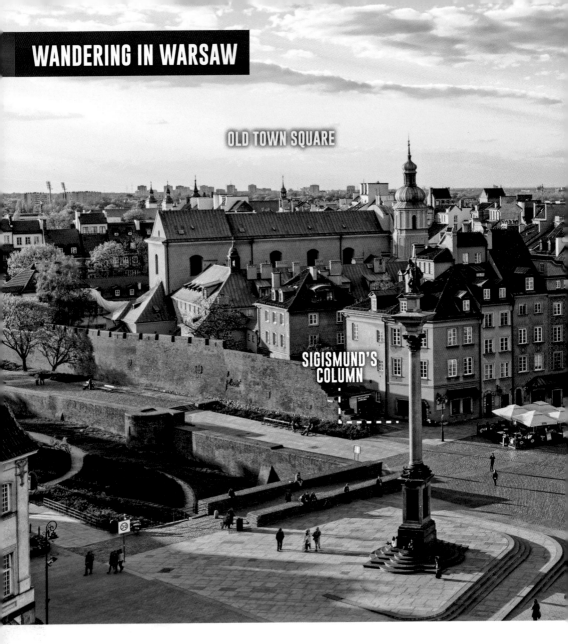

WANDERING IN WARSAW

OLD TOWN SQUARE

SIGISMUND'S COLUMN

After arriving by train, a family heads to Old Town to start their tour of Warsaw. They eat open-faced sandwiches at an outdoor café. Then, they explore a market filled with local crafts. They wander along the cobblestone streets and snap photos of the Royal Castle and Sigismund's Column.

OTHER TOP SITES

THE CLOTH HALL

ST. MARY'S CHURCH

TATRA NATIONAL PARK

WIELICZKA SALT MINE

The family spends the afternoon visiting the Copernicus Science Center. They learn from the displays on robots and energy before watching an amazing show at the planetarium. The family ends their day with a sunset cruise on the Vistula River. Welcome to Poland!

BALTIC SEA

GULF OF
GDAŃSK

RUSSIA

N
W   E
S

POZNAŃ

POLAND

GERMANY

WARSAW

WROCŁAW

ŁÓDŹ

KRAKÓW

CZECH REPUBLIC

SLOVAKIA

Poland is located in central Europe. It covers an area of 120,728 square miles (312,685 square kilometers). Warsaw, the capital city of Poland, lies in the nation's east.

Seven countries border Poland. To the east are Belarus and Ukraine. The country's southern neighbors are Slovakia and the Czech Republic. Germany borders Poland to the west. Waves from the Baltic Sea and the **Gulf** of Gdańsk crash against Poland's northern coastline. Kaliningrad, a small part of Russia, shares a border with Poland in the north. Lithuania is Poland's northeastern neighbor.

UKRAINE

LANDSCAPE AND CLIMATE

Most of Poland is relatively flat. There are sand **dunes** and swamps along the Baltic coast. South of the coast is a rocky area that has thousands of lakes. Many farms dot the central lowlands, which are part of the North European **Plain**. Hills and mountains span the southern edge of Poland. Jagged peaks rise in Tatra National Park. The Vistula and Oder are Poland's major rivers. They flow northward before emptying into the Baltic Sea.

= NORTH EUROPEAN PLAIN
= TATRA NATIONAL PARK

VISTULA RIVER

ODER RIVER

N
W—E
S

FANTASTIC FORESTS

Forests cover almost one-third of Poland. Beech, fir, spruce, and oak are all common trees throughout the country.

PIENINY MOUNTAINS

VISTULA RIVER

WARSAW
Average seasonal highs and lows

JANUARY
HIGH: 33 °F (1 °C)
LOW: 24 °F (-4 °C)

APRIL
HIGH: 56 °F (13 °C)
LOW: 39 °F (4 °C)

JULY
HIGH: 76 °F (24 °C)
LOW: 57 °F (14 °C)

OCTOBER
HIGH: 55 °F (13 °C)
LOW: 41 °F (5 °C)

°F = degrees Fahrenheit
°C = degrees Celsius

Poland's climate is **temperate**. There are several separate seasons. Snowy winters melt into sunny springs. Summers are mild and rainy. Autumn is sunny, then **humid** before winter.

Poland is home to many wild animals. In the waters of the Baltic Sea, European eels come out to feed on fish and shellfish at night. Red-breasted mergansers **migrate** along the coastal waters. They dive down to prey on small fish, such as gobies. The country's vast forests are home to many animals, including elk, deer, wisent, and wild pigs.

Goatlike animals called chamois move with ease on the steep slopes of Poland's southern mountains. Lynx, foxes, and eagles all hunt alpine marmots in their highland **habitat**. These furry rodents whistle alarm calls if they sense danger.

RED-BREASTED MERGANSER

ALPINE MARMOT

CHAMOIS

WONDERFUL WISENT

The wisent is Europe's largest land mammal. This type of bison nearly died out. The population grew from a small number of survivors in zoos. Now more than 2,000 wisent roam in the Białowieża Forest.

10

WHITE-TAILED
EAGLE

WHITE-TAILED
EAGLE

Life Span: 20 years
Red List Status: least concern

white-tailed eagle range =

LEAST CONCERN	NEAR THREATENED	VULNERABLE	ENDANGERED	CRITICALLY ENDANGERED	EXTINCT IN THE WILD	EXTINCT

Poland is home to over 38 million people. Most have **ancestors** from Poland. One smaller **ethnic** group is the Silesians. More than 2 million foreigners live in Poland. Many are **migrant workers** from Ukraine, Belarus, and Germany. Others are from Asian countries, including India and Vietnam. In recent years, Poland's population has been dropping. Women are having fewer children. Some Poles are also moving to other countries.

Most Poles are Catholic. Small numbers of people are Orthodox Christians or follow other religions. Polish is the nation's official language. German and English are also commonly spoken.

FAMOUS FACE

Name: **Robert Lewandowski**
Birthday: **August 21, 1988**
Hometown: **Warsaw, Poland**
Famous for: **Professional soccer player who was named the Best FIFA Men's Player in 2020**

SPEAK POLISH

ENGLISH	POLISH	HOW TO SAY IT
hello	cześć	CHESH-ch
goodbye	do widzenia	doe veed-ZEN-ya
please	proszę	PROH-shuh
thank you	dziękuję	jen-KOO-yuh
yes	tak	takh
no	nie	nyeh

ŁÓDŹ

WROCŁAW

GARDENS IN THE CITY

Many Polish cities have publicly owned gardens. City residents can grow fruits and vegetables for their families in their own little plots.

About three out of five Poles live in **urban** areas. Many people dwell in central Poland near Warsaw and Łódź. Warsaw is the country's largest city with over 1.5 million people. The region around the southern city of Kraków is also well-populated. Most people in Polish cities live in apartments, which they often own. Many urban families do not own cars. People use buses and trains to get around.

Most people in Poland's **rural** areas live in single-family homes. Poles in the countryside usually travel by bus or car.

Poland has a rich musical **tradition**. Many people consider the classical composer Frédéric Chopin to be Poland's most famous musician. Poles continue to listen to classical music. But they enjoy modern music, too. Polish rapper Taco Hemingway is quite popular. His songs tell of everyday people, life in the city, and other current topics.

TRADITIONAL POLISH CLOTHING

Each region of Poland has different traditional clothing. At many festivals, women wear colorful, flower-patterned skirts with ribbons. White shirts, embroidered vests, and a floral or cloth headdress complete the outfit. Men wear caps, pants, and decorated ja

Many types of folk art are created in Poland. Carved wooden sculptures, usually painted or stained, are common. Polish artist Magdalena Abakanowicz helped make fiber arts popular. Paintings and ceramics are also well-liked in Poland. Paper cuttings called *wycinanki* are **symmetrical** and usually very colorful.

Children in Poland must complete a year of preschool. They begin six years of primary school around age 7. Students attend **gymnasium** for three years after primary school. At age 16, some Poles train for specific careers at **vocational** schools. Others prepare to study at universities.

More than half of all Poles have **service jobs**. Some work in construction or at communications companies. Others have jobs in schools, banks, or the **tourism** industry. Polish factories produce cars, vehicle parts, furniture, and computers. Farmers grow grains and vegetables, such as potatoes and sugar beets. They also produce pork, eggs, and dairy products.

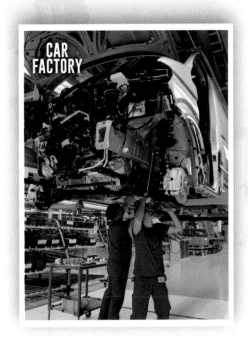

CAR FACTORY

SPECTACULAR SHIPS

Poles have built many kinds of ships throughout the nation's history. Today, building yachts is a booming business. Polish shipyards also produce cruise ships and ferries. Gdańsk is a major site of shipbuilding and repair.

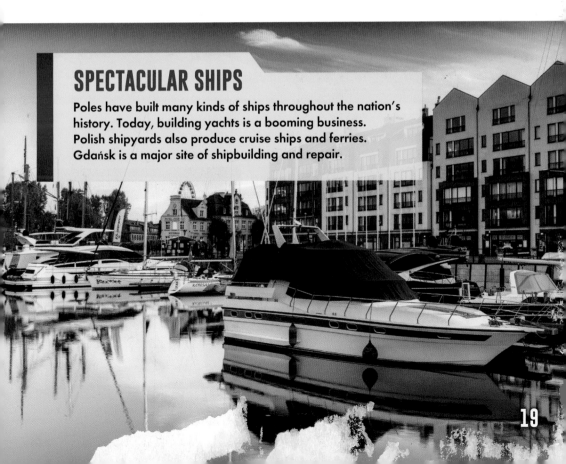

HIKING

Soccer is the most popular sport in Poland. It is played across the country by everyone from children to professional athletes. Many Poles also take part in track-and-field, skiing, volleyball, and basketball. Hiking and biking are common outdoor activities. Others kayak and canoe on Poland's rivers.

SOCCER

Gardening is a hobby enjoyed by many Poles. Millions of people also go mushroom picking in autumn. Poles often travel when they have time off from work and school. Many go to the Baltic coast, the mountains, or the lakes region. At home, Poles play video games and card games like bridge.

MUSHROOM PICKING

WYCINANKI

Wycinanki is a traditional Polish paper cutout. Common subjects include roosters and the tree of life. Feel free to create your own design!

What You Need:
- black and white construction paper
- colored construction paper (optional)
- chalk or a white crayon
- scissors
- glue

How to Make:
1. Fold your piece of black construction paper in half. Have the folded edge on the left and the open edge on the right.
2. Use your chalk or crayon to draw a design on the black paper.
3. Cut the design out, then unfold the paper so it lies flat.
4. Glue this paper cutting onto your piece of white paper.
5. If you want, you can cut out some pieces of colored paper to add detail to your wycinanki. Once it is dry, display it in a special place!

DELIGHTFUL DAIRY

Poles enjoy a wide variety of dairy. Kefir is a popular kind of milk, similar to a yogurt drink. Traditional cheeses are in many recipes. Dishes from breakfast to dessert include the white cheese called *twaróg*.

People in Poland often eat cereal, eggs, cheese, or open-faced sandwiches for breakfast. Cabbage is a key ingredient in many Polish meals. *Bigos* is a stew made of pickled cabbage, mushrooms, and sausage. Pork and cabbage is another popular dish. Many meals include soup. Red beet soup called *barszcz* and duck soup known as *czarnina* are commonly eaten.

No visit to Poland would be complete without *pierogi*. These dumplings are stuffed with meat or vegetables. Popular desserts in Poland include cheesecake and pastries. A favorite is *pączki*, a doughnutlike pastry often filled with jam or custard.

BIGOS

PIEROGI

RACUCHY Z JABŁKAMI

Make a light meal or snack of these Polish apple pancakes. Have an adult help you make them.

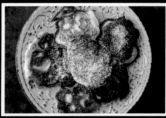

Ingredients:
1 3/4 cups milk
2 teaspoons active dry yeast
3 cups flour
2 tablespoons sugar
1/8 teaspoon salt
2 eggs
2 thinly sliced apples (Fuji or Gala are good choices)
3 tablespoons canola oil or vegetable shortening
powdered sugar (to decorate at serving time)

Steps:
1. Heat the milk on the stove or in the microwave until warm.

2. Stir the yeast in the warm milk until it is completely combined.

3. In a bowl, mix the flour, sugar, and salt. Pour in the yeast-milk mixture. Add the eggs and stir until combined. Let sit for 30 minutes in a warm place.

4. Fold the sliced apples into the batter until they are mixed in.

5. Warm the oil in a nonstick pan over medium heat. Use a large spoon or ice cream scoop to put the batter into the pan. Spread the batter out thinly so the pancakes are about 3 inches (8 centimeters) wide.

6. Fry for a few minutes until the top starts to look dry and the bottom is golden. Flip over and cook for another 2-3 minutes.

7. Put the pancakes on a plate and serve with powdered sugar. Enjoy!

FIRST DAY OF SPRING

Children in Poland often dress up in funny clothes on the first day of spring. Some skip classes. But it is a fun day at school with lots of games and no tests.

PISANKI

Many of Poland's biggest holidays are religious. On the Thursday before Lent, many Poles eat sweet foods like doughnuts. People often give up certain foods during the 40-day Lent period. Going to church and feasting with family are Easter traditions. Egg painting, known as *pisanki*, is another Easter activity.

The Christmas season begins with St. Nicholas bringing presents to children on December 6. Christmas Eve is celebrated with a feast. Families set an extra place at the table to welcome anyone in need. Poles celebrate their traditions and **culture** of generosity throughout the year!

CHRISTMAS
MARKET

1795
Prussia, Austria, and Russia take over all remaining Polish land, erasing the country of Poland for 123 years

AROUND 966
People in the region that is now Poland unite and become Christians under Mieszko I, the Duke of Poland

1939
Germany attacks Poland, which causes the start of World War II

1918
Poland becomes an independent country

1025
Bolesław I is crowned the first king of Poland

2004
Poland joins the European Union

1947
A communist government, supported by the Soviet Union, takes power

2017
Polish adventurer and national hero, Aleksander Doba, becomes the oldest person to kayak across the Atlantic Ocean

1989
Poland holds its first free and democratic elections in over 40 years

1992
Hanna Suchocka becomes Poland's first woman prime minister

POLAND FACTS

Official Name: Republic of Poland

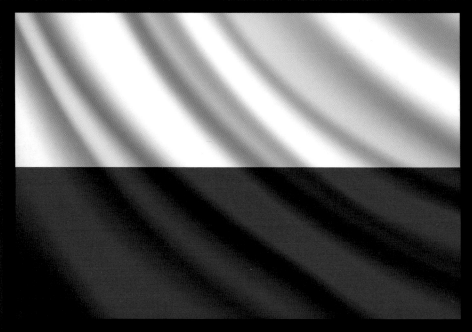

Flag of Poland: Poland's flag has two horizontal stripes. The top one is white and the bottom one is red. These colors have been used on Poland's coat of arms since the 13th century. The current flag was adopted in 1919.

Area: 120,728 square miles
(312,685 square kilometers)

Capital City: Warsaw

Important Cities: Kraków, Łódź,
Wrocław, Poznań

Population:
38,185,913 (July 2021)

COUNTRYSIDE
39.9%

WHERE
PEOPLE LIVE

CITY
60.1%

JOBS

- MANUFACTURING **30.4%**
- FARMING **12%**
- SERVICES **57.6%**

Main Exports:

cars

furniture

computers

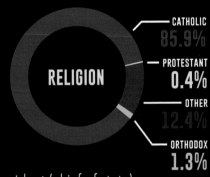

vehicle parts

National Holidays:
Constitution Day (May 3),
Independence Day (November 11)

Main Language:
Polish (official)

Form of Government:
parliamentary republic

Title for Country Leaders:
prime minister (head of government), president (chief of state)

RELIGION

- CATHOLIC **85.9%**
- PROTESTANT **0.4%**
- OTHER **12.4%**
- ORTHODOX **1.3%**

Unit of Money:
złoty

GLOSSARY

ancestors—relatives who lived long ago

culture—the beliefs, arts, and ways of life in a place or society

dunes—hills of sand

ethnic—related to a group of people who share customs and an identity

gulf—part of an ocean or sea that extends into land

gymnasium—a three-year middle school that follows primary school in Poland

habitat—land with certain types of plants, animals, and weather

humid—having a lot of wetness in the air

migrant workers—people who have moved to a new place for work

migrate—to travel from one place to another, often with the seasons

plain—a large area of flat land

rural—related to the countryside

service jobs—jobs that perform tasks for people or businesses

symmetrical—made up of exactly similar parts that face each other on opposite sides of a dividing line

temperate—a mild climate that does not have extreme heat or cold

tourism—the business of people traveling to visit other places

tradition—a custom, idea, or belief handed down from one generation to the next

urban—related to cities and city life

vocational—referring to a school that trains students to do specific jobs

TO LEARN MORE

AT THE LIBRARY

Klepeis, Alicia Z. *The Czech Republic*. Minneapolis, Minn.: Bellwether Media, Inc., 2021.

Mattern, Joanne. *Poland*. New York, N.Y.: Cavendish Square Publishing, 2020.

Murray, Julie. *Poland*. Minneapolis, Minn.: Abdo Publishing, 2018.

ON THE WEB

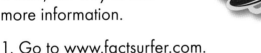

Factsurfer.com gives you a safe, fun way to find more information.

1. Go to www.factsurfer.com.

2. Enter "Poland" into the search box and click 🔍.

3. Select your book cover to see a list of related content.

INDEX

The images in this book are reproduced through the courtesy of: Ian Dagnall/ Alamy Stock Photo, front cover; fotorince, pp. 4-5; KerrysWorld, p. 5 (The Cloth Hall); Nightman1965, p. 5 (St. Mary's Church); Oleg Totskyi, p. 5 (Tatra National Park); Xseon, p. 5 (Wieliczka Salt Mine); Tomasz Warszewski, p. 8; Lukasz Engel, p. 9 (top); S-F, p. 9 (bottom); Dmytro Gilitukha, p. 10 (chamois); Bjoern Wylezich, p. 10 (red-breasted merganser); Astrid Gast, p. 10 (alpine marmot); Susann Moldenhauer, p. 10 (wisent); Rocchas, p. 11; aul Thompson Images/ Alamy Stock Photo, p. 12; Ververidis Vasilis, p. 13 (top); Mazur Travel, p. 13 (bottom); Traveller70, p. 14; Curioso.Photography, p. 15; Michal Ludwiczak, p. 16; Malgosia S, p. 17; Agencja Fotograficzna Caro/ Alamy Stock Photo, pp. 18, 19 (top); Patryk Kosmider, p. 19 (bottom); ewg3D, p. 20 (top); Dziurek - Sport/ Alamy Stock Photo, p. 20 (bottom); Aleksandra Tokarz, p. 20 (top); Agnieszka Murphy/ Alamy Stock Vector, p. 20 (bottom); Madzia71, p. 22; BBA Photography, p. 23 (top); Brent Hofacker, p. 23 (middle); vivooo, p. 23 (bottom); Studio Barcelona, p. 24; Credit:Travel_Motion, p. 25; INTERFOTO/ Alamy Stock Photo, p. 26; Unknown author (public domain)/ Wikipedia, p. 27; mkos83/ Getty Images, p. 29 (banknote); Andrew Duke/ Alamy Stock Photo, p. 29 (coin).